Creators
of the
Plains

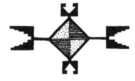

Thomas E. Mails

Illustrations by the Author

COUNCIL OAK BOOKS

Quotes are taken from the following books:

Bass, Althea. *The Arapaho Way, A Memoir of an Indian Boyhood.* Clarkson N. Potter, Inc., New York, 1966.

Brown, Joseph Epes. *The Sacred Pipe.* University of Oklahoma Press, Norman, 1953.

Catlin, George. *Letters and Notes on the Manners, Customs, and Condition of the North American Indians* (Vol. 1). Ross & Haines, Inc., Minneapolis, 1965.

Dodge, Col. Richard Irving. *Thirty-Three Years Among Our Wild Indians.* Archer House, Inc., New York, 1959.

Grant, Bruce. *American Indians Yesterday and Today.* E.P. Dutton & Co., Inc., New York, 1960.

Grinnell, George Bird. *The Cheyenne Indians, Their History and Ways of Life.* Cooper Square Publishers, Inc., New York, 1962.

_____. *The Story of the Indian.* D. Appleton and Co., New York, 1906.

Hofsinde, Robert. *Indian Warriors and Their Weapons.* William Morrow and Co., New York, 1965.

Lehmann, Herman. *Nine Years Among the Indians—1870-1879.* Von Boeckmann-Jones, Co., Printers, Austin, Texas, 1927.

Linderman, Frank B. *Plenty Coups, Chief of the Crows.* University of Nebraska Press, Lincoln, 1962.

Lowie, Robert H. *Indians of the Plains.* Natural History Press, Garden City, New York, 1963.

_____. *The Northern Shoshone.* American Museum of Natural History, New York, Jan. 1909.

Lyford, Carrie A. *Quill and Beadwork of the Western Sioux.* U.S. Dept. of the Interior, BIA, 1940.

Saloman, Julian H. *The Book of Indian Crafts and Indian Lore.* Harper and Row, Publishers, New York and Evanston, 1928.

Schultz, James Willard. *Blackfeet and Buffalo.* University of Oklahoma Press, Norman, 1962.

Tunis, Edwin. *Indians.* The World Publishing Company, Cleveland and New York, 1959.

Council Oak Books, Tulsa, OK 74120
Copyright © 1997 by Thomas E. Mails. All rights reserved.
Originally published in a slightly different version in
Mystic Warrotrs of the Plains. Copyright © 1972 by Thomas E. Mails.

01 00 99 98 97   5 4 3 2 1

Library of Congress cataloging-in-publication data
Mails, Thomas E.
    Creators of the Plains / Thomas E. Mails; illustrations by the author.
        p. cm. — (The Library of Native Peoples)
    "Originally published in a slightly different version in Mystic Warriors of the Plains.
        c1972, c1991"—CIP galley.
    ISBN 1-57178-047-5 (alk. paper)
    1. Indian Art—Great Plains. 2. Indians of North America—Great Plains— Industrues.
        I. Mails, Thomas E. Mystic Warriors of the Plains. II. Title. III. Series.
    E78.G73M33 1997
    704.03 ' 97078—dc21   97-12699
                                                            CIP

Edited and Designed by Tony Meisel, AM Publishing Services
Printed in the United States of America
ISBN 1-57178-047-5

Contents

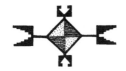

An Overview of Arts and Crafts 5

Painting 28

Quillwork and Beadwork 53

Shields 68

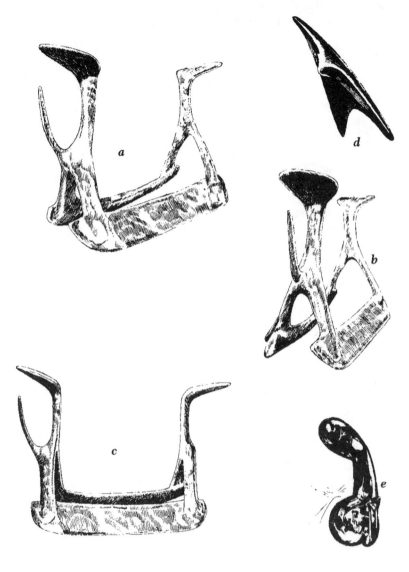

Plains woman's saddle as sculpture. *a, b,* and *c,* three views to show graceful design of saddle. *d* and *e,* contemporary metal sculptures for comparison with woman's saddle.

An Overview of
Arts and Crafts

The feeling of the Plains Indians toward their God was one of deepest reverence. They did not speak of loving Him, yet they looked to Him at all times, and in this sense lived in an atmosphere which was infused with the divine presence, which *is,* after all, a love relationship in itself!

Therefore, it is of some import to recognize that the Plains Indians' craftworks, including their weapons, were a result of what they had been shown in dreams and visions, and as such were in themselves a link with the Supreme Being. Something about the form and decoration of each piece always moved its owner beyond its earthly purpose. In a sense, considering the attitude and care employed in making any object, it may be said that he prayed his creations into their finished form. Thus it was inevitable that the piece he produced always enshrined a bit of each man in his heaven-earth relationship. And by the time he died, much of the story of his life could be read in the sum of the pieces he left behind.

Native American products, although greatly influenced in time by exposure to Anglo Saxon materials and ways, were an indigenous form of American art. Long before the entrance of foreign leaven, the Native Americans were well advanced in simple but diversified handicrafts. Most every piece they would ever use came into being in a simplified state early in their history and these items were only modified in form by the environmental needs and resources of the group as time passed. The skills acquired over the years and new possibilities which arose as they learned from and traded with the Whites only served to improve what already existed. The reason for this is plain. Their arts and industries utilized the mineral, vegetable, and animal products of nature. They copied directly from the plains over which they roamed, and from the sky under which they lived. Therefore, what they created was an imitation of nature, and it was usually done in an attempt to understand and adapt to the powers of the objects they were duplicating. Thus they reduced the items of heaven and earth which surrounded them to functional symbols. For example, many of their creations were what would be called textured collages today, as they were grand assemblages of wondrous items such as nuts, berries, bones, teeth, furs, skins, human and animal hair, feathers, and quills. Such items were not, however, assembled in a helter-skelter way. A dream or vision person told them what to use and where to put each piece. Every item had a special purpose, and played its part in the telling of a personal story.

Accordingly, while we find general resemblances to the primitive arts of other races, the art of the Plains Indian is so unique as to be worthy of extensive study. Naturally some people were more talented than others, but the spiritual way of life tended to produce the natural artist and craftsman. He, meaning both male and female, attained a mature reserve and dignity which endowed him with an unusual capacity for discipline and careful work. Upon examining his crafts today, one discovers that the Plains artist had innate taste, a naturally fine sense of line and rhythm, and a grand sense of texture and color; from it all

Above, side and back views of man's warbonnet. *Below*, warbonnet reduced to simple form for graphic illustration of sculptural qualities of bonnet.

evolved an art form peculiarly his own.

The approach precluded assembly line techniques. No two pieces were alike, and every item still in existence today is rare in that it is one of a kind. Mass production would have been an alien thought, for the Native American's work was really himself and for use in his daily life. It was never a piece of unnecessary bric-a-brac which would only be admired from a distance on occasion. It was a carefully formed and functional personal object of daily usefulness, and which, by its form and decoration, gave additional meaning to everything he experienced. In effect, Plains art was reverently coaxed, not forced, into being. The vital point was this: Every object served a threefold function. The first was to intensify the artist's spiritual feelings, the second was to play a utilitarian role in personal and community life, and the third was to be both mobile and durable.

All art, from forming to finish, was done in such a way as to bring the inanimate object to life in the mind of the artist. Animals and humans were drawn with their structure and life lines showing. Every piece the Native American made was detailed to show best against a blue sky or firelight, and when in motion; it was not for static showcase display. Sound too was made a part of most items. Tin cones, bells, and bags of loose stones were added to nearly every product, and the preferred sounds were those which came closest to being an echo of nature. In fact, the comparatively recent idea of achieving vision in motion was a natural part of the artist's approach on the Plains a hundred years ago. Therefore, the mobile quality of Plains art must be given its due, for not only did the finished piece itself have parts that moved, it was all easily movable from one place to another. The migrating civilizations of most other lands were forced to leave their cumbersome creations behind, but the Native American took his along with a minimum of effort and in a matter of minutes. No art has ever possessed a less static quality.

Many desirable features are found in Native American painting. If done by women it was similar to contemporary geometrical designs in form, and if by men, was realistic. They did this superbly well with pure vegetable and earth colors, painting on hides, wood, horses, and themselves!

One commonly reads that Native Americans were poor artists— that the Native American's ideas of art were "rude"; that he had an eye for bright colors, but no notion of drawing; his figures of men and animals were grotesque, and were as grotesquely painted in staring hues of red, yellow, and black, his paints being burned clays and charcoal. (Grinnell, *The Story of the Indian,* pp. 160-61) It is also said that "among the Plains Indians stone sculpture was absent and wood carving as a craft too little developed to foster artistry, as demonstrated by some ceremonial objects." (Lowie, *Indians of the Plains,* p.130)

Such views reveal a failure to understand the Native American's artistic purpose. Modern man lives in a billboard age wherein advertisements must be simple enough to be read at a distance by a passing motorist. It was precisely so in a mobile Plains society, since clothing and other objects had to be read and appreciated while people were on the move. It made no difference whether the village was shifting its location or encamped for the night, for once the caravan stopped, the people went into a more personal kind of motion—working, dancing, joining in society activities, or telling their animated stories. Therefore, Plains art evolved as a simple form, and remained so because it was

Mounted Nez Percé warrior illustrating artistic unity of warrior and horse.

perfect for its purpose! It was billboard art, the very art form of today's rapid reader, and a parallel to the history-changing art of the French impressionists in its intent.

For centuries the women dyed the quills of the porcupine, sewing them on garments, robes, and bags, wrapping pipestems with them, and weaving them into belts and arm bands. This was an art practiced nowhere else in the world, and so marvelously done it mystifies the one who sees it for the first time as to how they accomplished it.

Beads are not often thought of as valuable gifts, yet when traders and explorers brought them to the Plains, the women urged the men to trade for them, and then used them in spectacular ways on items which they had formerly done with quills. Sometimes they used them in combinations with quills. Each region, since nature was viewed through slightly different eyes by the individual tribes, developed its own style, color combinations, and sewing methods, so that an expert could sometimes tell the tribe it came from, and the approximate date it was made.

Native American artistry exhibits a sense of color, texture, mass balance, and sculptural form. It is a mistake to attempt to relocate any part of an Native American's design or object, for one soon finds that in doing so he has thrown it out of balance. Whether by rule or intuition, no one color overwhelms anything. A small spot of bright red paint on the right is compensated for by a large mass of gray feathers on the left. The color and mass selections were thus because they were made with great patience, and women were seen to spend hours experimenting with a single design.

Plains art included sculpture, and the Native Americans were masters in the use of natural roots and branches for society club emblems and medicine objects. To appreciate their sculptures, though, one must recognize that true sculpture results from the completed forming of any natural object—a matter in which the Plains artisan excelled. For example, if a woman's saddle is compared with pieces of contemporary sculpture, it is seen that such a saddle, or a man's headdress, if it were cast in bronze, would grace any museum's collection today, and it would look as if it were done by the finest modern sculptor. Since tactile qualities also made everything a delight to hold, it becomes even more evident that only an intensely sensitive being could have produced these, his wartime ferocity not in any case obviating the point. Besides the medicine and society club items, there were well-carved wooden musical instruments and stone pipes.

The quality of Plains Indian taxidermy was the highest, being not in the least excelled by modern methods.

Sewing with an awl and sinew, as executed by the women, was also a rare art in itself.

After the mid-nineteenth century the old techniques of horse painting were continued, but they were accompanied by beautiful pieces of horse gear. Beaded saddles, beaded martingales, cruppers, beaded stirrups, quilled head masks, quilled head decorations, and fancy bridles would sometimes nearly cover an animal. When a parade took place, the entire entourage was a splendid, mobile coronet, and in the early reservation period, horses and riders were so stately as to dazzle the imagination!

Clothing design itself was truly something, for not only the color and appendages, but also the cut of every part accommodated itself to the immediate actions and flamboyance of the Native American. War

Examples of Plains sculpture. *a*, bone flesher. *b*, woman's berrymasher hammer. *c*, ceremonial wooden carving of Crow Lumpwood Society. *d*, Arapaho ceremonial doll. *e*, horn spoon with beaded handle. *f*, Sauk-Fox ceremonial stick utilizing natural root. *g*, Tobacco Society sacred hoe made from root or branch with stone blade—24 inches long.

shirts were roomy and split on the sides to facilitate arm movements, or to permit sitting and riding with legs folded or bent. The absence of trouser seats eliminated binding. Fringes were placed so as to cause mobile shadow patterns as arms were raised. Split-tailed warbonnets and crow bustles hung magnificently down the horse's sides behind a mounted warrior. With a few exceptions, everything the Plains Indian made was featherlight, could be packed in a jiffy into an unbelievably small case, and then unfolded again in perfect shape and unharmed. Every part of his costume was pleasing and colorful, with this further quality—it was designed so that every angle presented something new. It follows, then, that any item in a museum should be on a rotating stand and exposed to steady breezes like those of the great prairies and plains.

After 1890, when the Native Americans were placed on reservations and materials were in short supply, crafts deteriorated in quality. In recent years the tendency has been toward the use of excessively gaudy colors and materials for costumes. It is only sensible that today's Native American dancers should be using today's materials. Yet the ancient products were harmonious, creative, reserved, and gracious to a fault, as any comparison will show, and the Native Americans themselves appreciated this no end. Many a warrior expressed his overwhelming admiration for an enemy's grand appearance; pausing, as only an Native American would do, to take this all in before engaging him in battle. Once, when moving onto a battlefield, Plenty Coups said, "I have never seen a more beautiful sight than our enemy presented . . . a young Sioux dashed from their line . . . his feathered war-bonnet blowing open and shut, open and shut in the wind, as he swung his body from one side to the other on his horse. He was riding a beautiful bay, with a black mane and tail, and fast." (Linderman, *Plenty Coups,* pp.257-58)

Prior to the receipt of metal tools from the Whites, all Plains implements were made of bone, wood, and stone. Many of these ancient pieces have been found, and others have been described by early travelers, yet we have only a limited knowledge of their suspected total variety. Much of the Plains style can be traced to the Eastern Woodland tribes, although the Plains type became distinctive in time, and a collector can learn to distinguish Plains items from those of other areas.

Native American women pounded chokecherries on a flat stone slab with a stone hammer called a "berrymasher," which was grooved round the middle of the stone and secured by wet rawhide passed around the groove and then wrapped and shrunken over a wooden handle. Mashers were also used to break up bones to extract the marrow. These were not war clubs. The stone heads of war clubs were sometimes mounted in a similar fashion, but as a rule they were thinner, oval or pointed at both ends. Large berrymashers were sometimes used for killing a wounded buffalo at the buffalo jumps, but that is as close as they came to contact with living things.

Water-worn pebbles and small shale slabs served as effective scrapers. Arrow shafts were smoothed between two grooved stones. Knives were of stone or bone; Coronado saw buffalo hunters cut meat with flint knives in 1541. In ancient times beautifully shaped arrow and lance heads were fashioned of stone, sinew, bone, and animal horns; although by the period under consideration metal points had been obtained in trade and stone points were no longer being made.

Pipe bowls were sculptured out of stone, especially of red catlinite. The Arapaho made black stone pipes, and the Blackfeet carved some of their bowls from a dark greenish stone which was found in their own territory.

Sharp and graceful bone awls were used to punch holes and then to push the sinew through them as the women sewed. Coronado's men also saw many of these in use. Investigators of old Pawnee dwelling sites have found fragments of perforated buffalo and elk ribs of a type known to be used for straightening arrow shafts. They have also found picks made of deer and buffalo bone which were used for digging. Very strong hoes were made from the shoulder blades of buffalo. Skin dressers employed several implements of bone, horn, and antlers, such as the

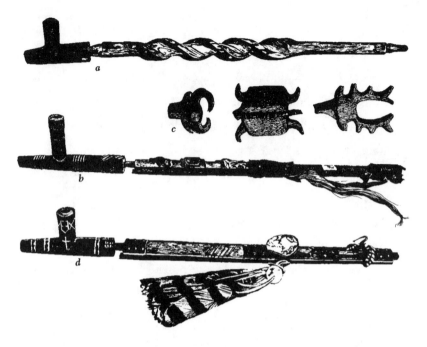

Pipes. *a*, carved spiral wood stem, probably Sioux. *b*, wood stem with carved animal symbols. *c*, enlargement of symbols. *d*, wooden stem with carved diagonal ridges and further adorned with brass tacks and sea shell.

gracefully shaped fleshers made from the foot bones of large game animals. Buffalo skins were scraped with adz-shaped, classic antler tools which were fitted in the historic period with iron blades.

Not many textile crafts were practiced on the Plains. With the buffalo and other animal hides so readily available they were not needed. Even most ropes were made of hide, although the Blackfeet twisted the tough bark of a certain shrub into rope, and the Omaha tribe pounded the fibers of a nettle until it was freed from the woody part, then braided it into rope. For storage bags, Omaha women doubled plaited fiber scarves and sewed them together at the sides. The men also used them to stow away their ceremonial articles. The Iowa tribe made loosely twined rectangular storage bags and floor mats from a basswood or nettle fiber. The Pawnees made woven fiber mats for floors, bedding, beds, curtains, and corpse wrappings. A Pawnee burial site was found to contain remnants of matting which showed a simple twining technique with narrow-leaved grass or rush fibers. The same excavation revealed bits of buffalo-hair cloth.

Soft, twilled buffalo-hair wallets were made by the southernmost Sioux, but the well-made twined woven pouches of the Blackfeet were imported from the marginal Plateau tribes.

Only the stationary villagers and the peripheral groups, such as the Utes, Shoshones, Mandans, Hidatsas, Arikaras, and Pawnees, made woven carrying baskets. Small, shallow basketry gambling trays made by the coiled technique were produced by the Pawnees, Arikaras, Mandans, Kiowas, Comanches, Cheyenne, and Arapaho.

The problems involved in the maintenance and transportation of earthenware pottery made its production undesirable for the migratory tribes. Recent archaeological findings reveal that the villagers of the upper Missouri did manufacture a few clay pots. But compared with the abundant ceramic ware of other areas there was little Plains pottery to be found, and what there was, was unadorned and undeveloped. Moreover, even the villagers lost their interest in the craft when the traders' metal utensils became available. As to construction, all Plains pottery was hand-molded. Cooking vessels were of one piece, as were the clay pipes of the Mandans. An identifying Pawnee feature was a collarlike rim on the pots with an incised ornamentation consisting mainly of isosceles triangles enclosing chevrons or lines parallel to one of the sides.

Some carpentry was practiced among the Plains Indians, and the skill shown in the fitting of the posts and beams of the Pawnee and Mandan earth lodges was commendable. The Plains tribes also made some unusual wooden carvings, such as three-dimensional representations of supernatural patrons.

In their sculpturing the Native Americans were particularly adept at utilizing the natural shape and grain of the wood. The stationary village men manufactured a number of wooden kitchen articles, including mortars and bowls. The Omahas shaped a one-by-three-foot grinding mortar from a section of a tree trunk, chipping one end to a point for insertion into the ground, and hollowing out the opposite end. Coals placed on the hollowed surface were fanned until they burned a basin in the wood. This was followed by smoothing the mortar with sandstone and water. A huge pestle, larger at the top than at the tapering end, completed the mortar and pestle working unit.

The Omahas made their dinner bowls from black walnut burs, the hollowing process being the same as that just given for the mortars. Plains ladles in general were made so that the handle could be hooked over the rim of the bowl. Spoons were gracefully shaped of wood and horn and the handles were quilled or beaded. Wooden bowls were made for mixing tobacco seeds, for holding paint, and for throwing dice in games. Ladders were made of notched logs, and a Hidatsa woman ascended to the top of her corn-drying racks on a notched cottonwood tree trunk which had been pointed and driven into the ground at the butt end.

Smoking pipes were carved in many different shapes and were made from various materials. The oldest were straight tubes of animal legbone or stone and were wrapped with sinew for added strength. Later models

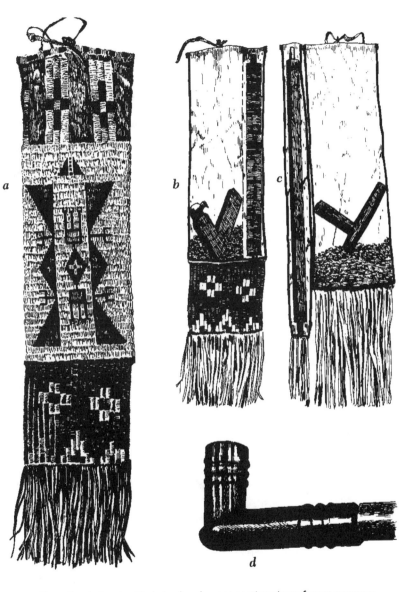

a, Sioux beaded and quilled pipe bag. *b*, cross-section view of most common Plains bag showing compartment for stem and how pipe bowl and tobacco were kept. *c*, cross-section view of less common two-compartment bag— bag shown is Ute. *d*, L-shaped catlinite pipe bowl—oldest style.

were curved, and some had their bowls set in an L shape at right angles to the stem. A T-shaped pipe bowl made of stone was the type most commonly used on the Plains. Many stone pipe heads were carved in the shape of geometric designs, or of animals or birds. The Osage pipe had a disk-shaped head, and the northernmost tribes used a unique stubby head called the Micmac. As the years passed, hardwood, bone, clay, and stone were all used for making pipe bowls. To make a clay bowl, blocks of hard, tough clay were carved out to make the outer shape and rubbed with fat or tallow. Then stone bow drills were used to make the holes. After this the bowls were hardened over a fire, and as they were smoked hardened further.

Stone pipe bowls were made from steatite, argillite, shale, limestone, serpentine slate, and catlinite. The last named was a soft red stone found in the well known pipestone quarries of the southwestern Minnesota area. These quarries were sacred ground to the Otto tribe as early as A.D. 1600, and the Sioux began using them about 1700. Tradition has it that the quarries were regarded as neutral ground by all of the tribes. Catlinite stone could easily be worked with flint or knife. White traders took advantage of the Native American's beliefs and the catlinite's soft, shaly deposits, and turned out thousands of pipes on lathes for the Native American trade. The stone and quarry received its name from George Catlin, who was the first White man to describe it to others in writings.

Most pipestems were made from ash or sumac, which had a soft pith in their center that could be easily removed. In the oldest method of making a stem, the wood was split, the pith scraped out, and the split pieces were glued and bound together. An elaborate plating of quillwork and wrappings of hide and fur were often added for decoration, and they helped to hold the two parts together. In trade days the pith core was removed with a red-hot wire. Another method said to have been used in the old days was to drill a small hole in the pith at one end of the stick, into which a wood-boring grub was inserted and the end sealed. The stick was then heated over a fire, and the grub, following the line of least resistance, would bore his way through the pith to make his escape.

The length of the average wooden pipe including the bowl was thirty inches, although some great ceremonial pipes were five feet long. Most wooden stems were broad and nearly flat in section. The catlinite stems were either round or oblong in cross section.

Beaded and/or quilled pipe bags were among the finest items made by the Native Americans. Their tobacco was carried in the bottom of the bag. The pipe bowl was separated from the stem when it was carried in the bag. Some bags had a stitched separation to provide a narrow side pocket for the stem. Ute bags had an entirely separate compartment for it. A thong drawstring tie was attached to the top of all pipe bags to secure the contents of the bag.

The Native Americans made an incredible variety of small pouches for every conceivable purpose. There were medicine bags which were easily identified as such by their long legs. There were small beaded amulet bags to be worn on a cord around the neck. And there were beaded belt pouches of many kinds. There was a beaded type known as a strike-a-light bag, in which flint and steel were carried—tin bells on the bottom and flap were standard decorations for these—and there were flat ration card bags used during the trading post days. Medicine bags could always be recognized by their scalloped and beaded top or bottom edges. Other bags were cut straight across. Small bags were often

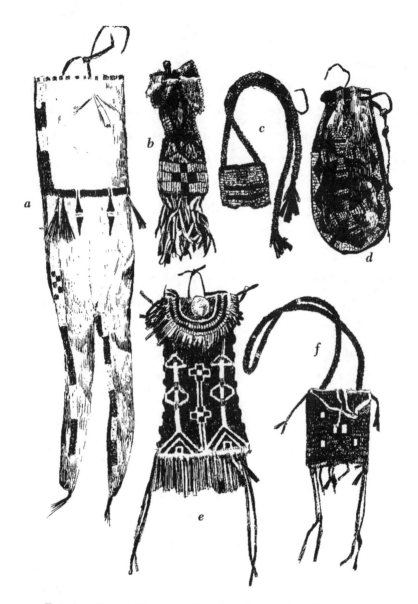

Typical small beaded bags. *a*, medicine bag, 15 inches long. *b*, small medicine bag of type worn on thong around neck. *c*, beaded top of awl case. *d*, southern Plains pouch for general purposes. *e*, strike-a-light bag to carry flint and steel. *f*, ration ticket pouch used during reservation period.

left plain on the back, although some of the better ones were beaded on both sides. In the latter case the two sides always had entirely different designs—but using the same colored beads or quills.

The variety of Plains musical instruments was very limited, and once again because of the mobility requirements. However, the ones that were made were gracefully done pieces of art.

The smallest musical instrument was the eagle wing bone whistle. It was sometimes left plain, yet often decorated with paint, quills, beads, beaded pendants, and eagle down, and worn suspended by a cord from the neck or the shirt front. A variation mentioned by Catlin was a turkey leg bone war whistle, but eagle bones were also used for that purpose. The tone was something like the cry of an eagle, and either end could be blown to produce a different tone for battle commands.

There was also an instrument called a flageolet which could produce a single sharp note. These were long tubular flutes of ash, the lower end carved, shaped, and painted to portray a crane's head with opened beak, and they were often carried by grass dancers. Men who dreamed of buffalo carved a larger and more elaborate twisted flute made of two grooved cedar halves glued together and bound by rawhide lashings. These were equipped with five finger holes and an air vent covered with an adjustable block for changing the pitch. They were decorated with a red paint stripe around each of the holes. A plainer version was embellished with floral symbols. Both types were used as love medicines, whose main purpose was to woo young maidens. However, men also played them in their lodges in the evening, and it is said they had a pleasant minor, lilting, whistling tone.

All societies had their rattles. A favorite type had two small buffalo

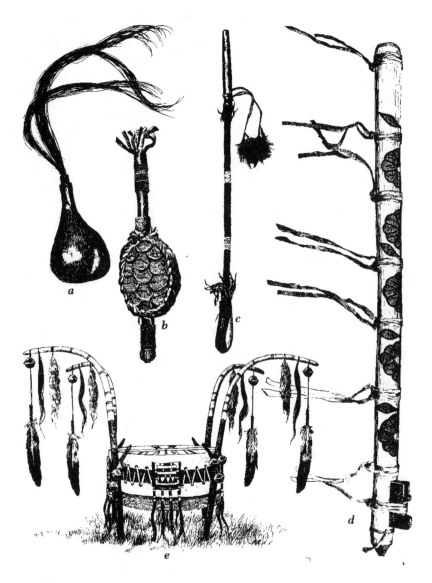

Musical instruments. *a*, deer hide rattle with horsehair pendant. *b*, turtle shell rattle. *c*, drum beater with beaded handle. *d*, wooden flute with rawhide fringes (34 inches long). *e*, four-man drum.

horns separated by a hollow hide tube, in which loose stones were placed. One horn was painted black and the other was painted red. Black horsehair was tied or glued to each of the horn tips. The most common type of rattle was made of deer hide. The hide was soaked, filled with sand, and left to dry. The sand was then emptied out, and the hide was filled with round pebbles collected from an anthill. A wooden handle was inserted and it was decorated with paint, symbols, and feathers. The buffalo scrotum made an excellent rattle which was used by holy men and doctors. Gourds made fragile and short-lived rattles, but they had a good tone. Tortoise shells with deer dewclaws tied to them as knockers were used for dances, and were strapped to the dancers' legs. A stick wrapped with deerskin, to which was attached, in rows, the cut and carved claws of a deer, was also used for society ceremonial purposes. Claws like this on a rawhide bandoleer were worn over the shoulders of dancers.

The Crows, Hidatsas and Utes, as well as other tribes, made rasps out of long flat boards by cutting deep notches along the top edge. A stick made of wood or bone was drawn backward and forward along the notches to make a rasping sound to accompany dances. Some of the rasps had snake or animal heads carved at one end and were trimmed to a point at the other.

To make a drum, flat willow boards were bent and shaped to make a circular frame. Then a piece of wet untanned deerskin was stretched over this and laced on, after which carrying straps were added. Men often painted symbolic designs, such as the sun or the four directions, upon their drums, though in some cases drumheads were undecorated. A type of large double-headed drum peculiar to the Plains was built by cutting a section of a hollowed log, putting a hide head on it, and suspending it from the ground by four gracefully bent and decorated sticks. It was used for public ceremonies and dances since as many as four men could play it at once. To make even larger drums a full buffalo hide was stretched between wooden pegs a few inches above the ground. Drum beaters were made by covering the end of a short stick with a stuffed deerskin pad. The Warrior Societies decorated the handles of theirs with porcupine quillwork or with beads. Before they were played, drums were warmed over a fire to tighten the hide and to give them a richer tone, since damp weather loosened the head and affected the tone a great deal.

It is apparent, as one moves into the field of Plains Indian arts and crafts, that art forms of considerable significance are being encountered. Their creations, while primarily utilitarian, actually played roles in every area of personal and tribal life. They literally grew out of dreams and visions which resulted from the Native American's contact with God, with the ground, the trees, the air, and the visible and invisible creatures of the heavens and earth. Thus they were formed, indeed sculpted, with emotion and with a rare sensitivity to their ultimate purposes. Beyond this they were mobile in the highest degree, and when it came to garments, many were breath-taking in form, texture, color, and grace. The range of creations was broader by far than that for which the Native Americans are usually given credit, and a creativeness is revealed which deserves the world's highest respect. Above all, each piece was one of a kind, deeply personal, and when one advances to the point where he can read their shapes and designs he finds that a segment of a Native American's life has been enshrined in each of the things he or she has made. Discovering Native American art is, to say the least, an experience!

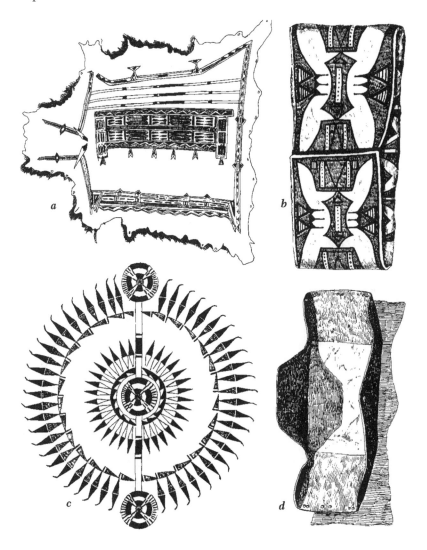

a, woman's painted buffalo robe. *b,* painted parfleche container—averaging 30 or so inches long when folded. *c,* man's "black warbonnet" robe design. *d,* method of folding parfleche.

Painting

Next to the dressing and sewing of skins, painting was probably the oldest of the major Native American arts or crafts. Certainly it dated back to prehistoric times, for Coronado learned of skin painting in 1540, and early traders and explorers found the Blackfeet already living in painted lodges and wearing painted buffalo robes.

The materials used in painting could be readily obtained anywhere in the Plains country. Native paints were derived from animal, vegetable, and mineral sources, with earth paints being the most common kind. An object can be dated by the color of its paint, for the earliest colors included only brown, red, yellow, black, blue, green, and white. Other colors indicate a later, nineteenth-century date. The Blackfeet discovered a half-dozen different reds, which provided them with colors of several hues and intensities. The base for red paints were crimson colored earth and a crushed, pale, reddish-yellow rock. A reddish brown could be obtained by baking gray or yellowish clay over ashes until it turned red. In the spring of the year the buds of the pussy willow were picked, kept overnight, and made into still another red paint. A yellow-colored earth was found beside the Yellowstone River. Yellow was also obtained from bull berries and the moss on pine trees. Buffalo gallstones provided yet another yellow. For blue the Native American artists used a duck manure from the lakes of country where wild ducks were plentiful. It was dried in the sun and then mixed with water. The early Native Americans were inclined to use the same color names for both blue and green, although they readily recognized the difference between the two colors, and affirm that their people used both "in the old days." Green came from copper ores, from a colored mud, or from plants growing near lakes. Some Native Americans reported they also knew how to mix

Man's painted war record buffalo robe.

a native blue mud and yellow to make green. White paint was obtained from white earth and from grinding down white clay. Lewis and Clark named the present Beaver Creek near Helena, Montana, which they passed in 1805, White Earth Creek, because they learned the Native Americans were accustomed to dig white paint beside it. Authorities say that white was obtained from selenite stone, which was heated and formed into a fine white powder. It was mixed with water to whiten buckskin garments and skin tipis. Powdered, charred wood and black earth provided black paint.

Of all the colors, red was used most in painting. Red earth was applied liberally to the surfaces of sacred objects used in ceremonials and to the Native American's face and body. Ceremonial bundles often contained a number of sacred objects which were completely covered with red paint.

Some powdered paints—one a dark-brownish red—were even used as a remedy for eczema, for eruptions of the skin, and for protection of the skin in frosty weather.

A variety of dyes were obtained from vegetable juices and roots.

Vermilion paint was one of the articles which was eagerly sought from the White traders, and the Native Americans paid nearly any price to procure it for ceremonial uses.

The trader Alexander Henry listed ten different pigments employed by the Piegan division of the Blackfeet in "painting and daubing their garments, bodies and faces" in the early years of the nineteenth century. (Henry, *New Light on the Early History of the Greater Northwest*) It is possible that some of them were colors obtained from the traders. During the reservation period commercial paints gradually replaced most of the original earth and vegetable colors.

To prepare them for use, the native pigments were baked to a powder over a fire, then ground in small stone or wooden mortars and mixed with tallow (Lowie speaks of mixing with a "gluey material"). (Lowie, *Indians of the Plains,* p.130) When the grinding was finished, each color was kept separately in a small buckskin bag closed at the neck by a buckskin thong or drawstring. When the artist was ready to use the paints, he mixed them with hot water, or with glue extracted by boiling in water the tail of a beaver or the white, clean underscrapings of a hide. The standard mixing bowls were very small turtle shells, clam shells, sherds, wood or stone cups.

Truly to appreciate the Native American artist's talent, one must consider that he worked with limited tools. His kit contained a number of straight, peeled willow branches of different lengths which served as rulers for painting straight lines. Some outfits included one or more short, flattened sticks for marking guidelines on a hide by pressure alone. Every toolbox had a number of chewed cottonwood or willow sticks for applying color, and the most preferred brushes were cut from the porous edge of a buffalo's shoulder blade or the end of his hipbone. The honeycomb composition of the bone brushes enabled them to hold the paint and permitted it to flow smoothly onto the hide surfaces. Thin, sharp bones were used for outlining and for painting fine lines, while other bones were rounded for spreading color over larger areas. Either the sides of the large bone brushes or else hollow bones which were loaded with paint and then blown were used for filling in the larger masses. The painter's fingers were also used for this purpose. In the last part of the nineteenth century a tuft of antelope hair was mounted on a

a, porous bone brushes. *b,* small hollowed stone mixing bowl. *c,* turtle shell mixing bowl. *d,* bone brush for laying in large areas. *e,* willow branch for painting straight lines. *f,* buckskin bags for paint. *g,* small bone brush. *h,* pointed stick for sharp lines. *i,* using fingers for broad lines. *j,* hollow bone used to blow paint on large areas.

stick in imitation of the White man's brushes. Then a separate brush was employed for each color.

American artists used no sketches or patterns. They organized their designs as they proceeded, measuring the outlines with peeled willow sticks of different lengths. Once, when asked how she selected her color combinations, a woman held up a yellow flower with a purple center, saying. "See, that is how the Great Spirit does it!" (Royce, *Burbank Among the Indians*, pp. 204-05)

The Hidatsas pressed the entire design into the hide, spread the paint over the impressions with the brush, and finally set the paint with a sizing of glue. Glue was also employed to outline the patterns, and could be used without colors on the various parts of a hide.

Early Dakota informants said that patterns were originally scraped into the skin. To accomplish this, the artist would scrape away portions of the pigmented layer of the buffalo skin, leaving sections of lighter or darker shading. Rare specimens of this technique can be seen today in some museums.

Most sizing consisted of thin glue made from beaver tail or skin scrapings boiled in water, but it was also obtained in the southern plains from the juice of crushed prickly pear leaves. After the Blackfeet obtained rice from the Whites they made a glue of it as well. The buffalo hides, having been scraped and treated with brains until they were smooth and soft, were also bone-white, and the application of the transparent mordant allowed the white to show through.

In the ordinary approach, the hide to be decorated was stretched and pegged hair side down on the ground, and the artist crouched or kneeled over it to work. Sometimes he or she was aided by one or more colleagues, especially on large surfaces and in pictographic drawings. A big hide might be placed on a vertical frame to facilitate the task. In painting a robe, a Sioux woman was seen to ply a creasing stick on the stretched and dampened hide. First she marked the outline of the border. Then, using tiny bone brushes, she applied her border color. Ordinarily, a single color was used for this. When the border was

Language of the men's robe. *a,* manner worn to address audience. *b,* manner employed to illustrate change of attitude. *c,* manner used to indicate meditation. *d,* manner of illustrating anger. Additional traditional forms were used to illustrate other attitudes.

completely filled in, she painted the central portion with larger bones, creasing the outlines first and then coloring. In frescolike technique, she kept the robe damp while painting. Mixing the paint with hot water alone caused it to soak into the damp hide and permanently fixed it after it had dried. Sizing the painting helped to preserve it further, gave it a gloss, and moreover had the pleasing effect of outlining the designs in white. One could pour water over it after the glue dried and the paint would not run.

The most favored articles for painting by women were their rawhide parfleche storage and carrying cases, which were usually made in pairs. The hides were painted before the cases were cut out—when completed, the pair was suspended lengthwise on the horse at each side by rawhide cords passed through burned holes in the margins of the cases, and then over the pommel and cantle of the packsaddle. The contents of these remarkable cases remained dry even when the Native

Americans were traveling in the hardest rain.

A number of smaller, rectangular or tubular cases were made from a single piece of rawhide and painted in the same manner as parfleches. As a rule, these cases were rounded or folded twice, stitched up the sides, and closed by a round or triangular flap over each end. The top was fastened in a clever manner by a thong passing through holes in the front of the case and tied. Cases intended to hold sacred medicine objects and bonnets can be identified by the long fringes at their sides or bottom. Others, without fringes, were used to carry such common household articles as skin dressing tools or the stone-headed berrymashers. Usually, cases were painted only on the front side, and with a geometric design.

Buffalo robes were the next most painted items, and easily the most glamorous pieces of work. In certain instances the decorative designs painted and/or quilled on the robe proclaimed the status of the wearer. They also designated the sex, to a certain degree the age, and whether the wearer was married or single. All clothing, as a matter of fact, served, in addition to its decorative and protective function, to distinguish one person from another. Unmarried women's robes were often embellished with a row of medallions and pendants across the bottom, while young, unmarried men wore robes with horizontal bands of quilling with four large medallions, the first medallion being placed at the left or head of the hide.

The Native American women painted geometric figures on their robes. A typical woman's robe employed horizontal quill stripes or a frame around an oblong field, which in turn enclosed many minor figures, and was in a characteristic position above the center. Buffalo

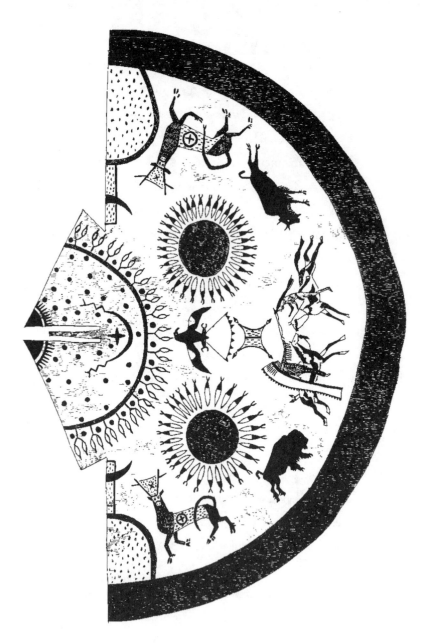

Ancient buffalo-hide tipi with warbonnet, bird and animal figures resulting from vision.

Ancient buffalo-hide tipi showing exceptional grace and creativeness of designs employed.

were popular symbols with women, as were two facing E's, each with four bars.

The characteristic man's robe of northern Plains tribes was painted or quilled with a stunning "black warbonnet" pattern which consisted of concentric circles with numerous small radiating figures each composed of two isosceles triangles and designated by the Native Americans as "feathers." The Comanches and their southern neighbors used a frame with a central hourglass pattern enclosing minor designs.

In addition to what was called the "marked male robe," every warrior of note had a "war record" robe on which he pictured his accomplishments in raiding and war. In doing war robes, all Native American men painted what are best described as naturalistic or realistic figures of warriors, horses, buffalo, and other animals. The figures were always bold, simple, shown in profile, and without background. Sometimes a man added a few geometric designs to his naturalistic figures.

A man either decorated his own robe or secured the services of a more skilled painter to do it for him. By tradition, when painting war history robes, only hot water was mixed with the paint and the figures were made freehand with a bone brush. Some artists painted the robe figures in outline alone, others worked in solid monochrome, and some used many colors. Red was the favored hue, but yellow and blue were also very popular. Careful study reveals that the figures were placed on the surface of the robe in an orderly composition. The Native American mind was incapable of unharmonious relationships, and balance always resulted. If one attempts to shift or remove just one figure from any robe it is soon seen that this is resoundingly true! Again, while robe painting has been called "more properly picture writing than art," it should be remembered that simple pictorial shorthand served marvelously to tell those who were familiar with the language of the painted figures exactly what a brave man's claims to distinction were; it indicated, with great economy and force of line, the number of horses he had stolen from enemy camps on each war party, the number of enemy weapons or other personal equipment he had taken, the number of the enemy he had killed or wounded, and the number of times he had served in the responsible position of leader of a war party or as a scout. Still, aesthetics is surely central to their work, for Native Americans were deeply impressed with the grace and beauty of their decorated robes, and they commented frequently upon them in their recollections. Indeed, they are noteworthy both for their informative and their aesthetic qualities, and the influences of White artists did not improve them. Critics have declared that compared with the semi-realistic, decorative figures painted by Cheyenne and Teton Dakota artists during the latter part of the nineteenth century, most earlier figures are but crude suggestions of living forms, human or animal. Yet the added detail actually tended to blunt the visual impact of the older work, for one cannot "read" a complex drawing while its wearer is in motion.

Robes were worn or carried in traditional ways, and had a language all their own. A speaker wore it one way when he was addressing an audience, another to show a change of attitude, another to indicate meditation, and another to display anger. (Omahas, BAE 27th Report, pp. 358-62) By tradition the head of the buffalo was worn to the left when the robe was wrapped around its owner, and all paintings were done with the "lay" of the robe in mind. Young men often wore their robes over their heads if they were courting, while older men placed one end under their right arm and held it with their left hand, leaving the right arm free. Women wore them over their heads at ceremonies.

The most remarkable and awe-inspiring of all Plains Indian paintings were the larger-than-life-size murals of animals which they painted on the conical outer walls of their lodge covers. Those of the Blackfeet were first mentioned by Alexander Henry, the fur trader, in 1809. He stated that both beasts and birds were represented in the paintings, and that buffalo and bears in particular were frequently delineated. A study of photographs and older paintings by White artists reveals that little or no change in the figure styles for lodges took place over the years.

Lodge paintings were more than decoration. Those who were versed

Left, Blackfoot artist laying in outlines of tipi painting. *Right,* Blackfoot artist painting buffalo hide stretched on frame rack.

in the traditions of their people found each painting to be more replete with religious and historical symbolism than a large stained glass church window is today. There were only a few gloriously painted lodges in each camp, since these were the residences of the leading men and of societies, or the places of tribal ceremonial functions—but of those so decorated, each had its fascinating legend to explain how its owner obtained the symbols and colors. According to the legends, all of the designs were given to their first human owners in dreams or visions. In these, the original animal owner of the lodge appeared to the sleeper and promised to give him his own painted lodge and the other sacred objects—which together were to be the sources of his supernatural power. The animal owner told the sleeping or transfixed man how to paint the lodge and how to assemble and shape the other sacred objects which would be associated with it. When he awoke, the man always followed these instructions to the letter. Therefore, each painted lodge became part of a complex of religious objects belonging to its owner. So long as he possessed it, he had certain rituals to perform and taboos to recognize. Whenever he sold his painted lodge to another, an elaborate transfer ritual had to be performed. And although Blackfoot painted lodges were frequently transferred from one owner to another within the three tribes, Blackfeet, Piegans, and Bloods, only the rightful owner was permitted to make use of the animal figures that belonged to his lodge. No other man dared copy them.

When a painted tipi cover became old and worn, the paintings on it were duplicated on a new one. Ordinarily, this was done in the fall of the year, just after the last tribal hunt when all the new lodge covers of the village were made. For the preliminary work the new lodge cover was

Painted tipis and designs. *a*, Blackfoot. *b*, Cheyenne. *c*, Sioux. *d*, Crow. *e*, tipi liner designs. *f*, pictographic styles used for figures employed on liners and tipi walls.

stretched into shape around the lodge poles. Usually the owner employed the services of a skilled artist and told him what to paint as he drew the outline of the forms in black paint, using red willow sticks for rulers and bone paintbrushes. All outlining was done while the lodge was standing, and the old painted lodge was set up nearby so the size and arrangement of its paintings could be referred to. When the skilled artist was finished, the new lodge cover was taken down and spread out flat on the ground. At this point the owner invited a group of people of "good reputation" to his lodge for a smoke. Working in a leisurely fashion, they helped him finish the painting, using buffalo tails or handfuls of long buffalo hair to apply the paint to the larger masses. The paint for lodges was mixed with hot water and rubbed onto the cover with considerable pressure. When the painting was finished the new lodge was erected again, and all of the ornaments which had hung on the old lodge were transferred to it. Then the owners of the other painted lodges in the camp were invited to gather inside the new lodge. Everyone prayed for God's blessings upon the lodge, and then they assisted the owner in the building of a purification sweat lodge nearby. When he had completed the sweat rite the ceremony of transferring the sacred symbols from the old to the new lodge cover was considered finished.

The old painted cover was disposed of either by taking it to a lake and weighting it with stones so that it would sink, or by spreading it out on the open plains. In the first instance the cover was given as an offering to the water spirits; in the second, it was an offering to the sun. Unpainted covers were simply cut up to make clothing and storage items.

Wild animal figures were stylized and decorative in form. Usually the body was a plain solid color; either black, blue, red, or yellow, but some of them were further detailed with representations of the throat, heart, and kidneys, which were believed to be the sources of energy of the animals depicted.

Many professional lodge painters employed what is best described as a straightforward composition of the upper and lower portions of the cover. At the bottom, a banded area two or more feet in height was often painted red to represent the earth. Within this area were one or two rows of unpainted circles to depict fallen stars. A row of triangular or rounded projections upward from the band appeared on a number of lodge covers, and these represented rounded hills or sharp mountain peaks. A banded area at the top of the cover, including the projecting ears or wind flaps, was sometimes painted black to symbolize the night sky. Arrangements of unpainted ovals within this area represented the constellations of the Great Bear and the Pleiades. A Maltese cross placed on the west side of the top was said to indicate the morning star, or butterfly, and was believed to bring powerful dreams to the lodge owner.

Painted tipi covers often had geometric borders at the top and the bottom with naturalistic pictures in the middle to show the exploits of the owners. Chief Satanta of the Kiowas had an entirely red tipi with red streamers at the end of poles atop it. Tipis with battle pictures were known as heraldic tipis. A spectacular Sioux tipi of particular note had its north side ornamented with battle pictures, while the southern half was painted with alternating horizontal stripes of black and yellow.

The Native Americans used large, buffalo skin draft liners that circled the inside of the tipi and provided an air barrier to insulate the lower portions of lodges. Most of these were painted with bright geometric designs by women. Among the Blackfeet, liner paintings were confined to a long, narrow, horizontal band near the top of the item, and to additional vertical bands projecting downward from the top band at intervals of about fifteen inches. An exception to the above was that men with outstanding war records were permitted to paint their lodge linings with pictographic representations of their deeds of valor, and in so doing used them for personal historical records.

Another painting use of real significance was the pictographic signature which served to identify an individual by name. When a scout was separated from his war party or camp, he could draw his signature,

Crow scout White Man Runs Him showing typical method of applying face paint.

couple it with other pictographs indicating his recent actions, and add a small arrow indicating his direction of movement, leaving the depiction on a rock, a piece of bone, skin, or cloth in a place where others of his tribe could find it, and thus learn what he had done and where he was going. Most tribes also kept pictographic calendar hides on which were set forth the outstanding tribal events of successive years.

However they were employed, the commonest figures in all male paintings were those of horses, men, and weapons drawn as they appeared in war or hunting. Next came religious symbols and a few buffalo. It should be mentioned that while war pictographs often show men regally dressed, that was usually done to identify the warrior. Except for premeditated engagements, warriors wore the lightest and plainest clothing possible while traveling so as not to be impeded by the weight.

Except for the huge tipi paintings, composition involved relatively small scenes. If the idea of perspective drawing ever occurred to the Plains artist, he deliberately put it away. Distant figures were frequently placed behind or above closer ones without a reduction in size, since in the artist's mind all of the figures were equally important.

It is apparent that composition was employed, and that the artist made every attempt to unify all of the scenes of a hide. In fact, they are very well balanced, and there is every reason to conclude that religious harmony led the Native American artist to employ by intuition the same rules as are used today for color and layout. Considering the Native Americans' educational and technical limitations, many of the pictographs displayed an enviable dynamic quality. The work was exciting, to say the least, and as good for its purpose as that which an enlightened nation has conceived of since. Old Plains painting was the epitome of visual contact, simultaneously calling into play communication, religious expression, and beauty.

The study of Plains painting is only complete when self-painting has been considered. For when a Native American was fortunate enough to have a multitude of colors, he painted his face in stripes and spots, in any style to please his individual but Spirit-guided attitude. A common face paint method was to use the finger tips or pointed sticks to paint cheek stripes from an eighth to a quarter of an inch in width vertically, or horizontally by starting at the nose, then running across to the ears, using red, yellow, blue, green, and as many other tints as one could procure. The forehead was striped in the same manner, with the lines running up and down. When the face was painted with spots, the pigments were daubed on with the fingers or paint tools. In all cases the paint was applied with forethought and purpose.

Men painted their faces regularly for protection against wind, sun, snow, and insects. When painting for this purpose the Native American first rubbed grease made from bear or buffalo back fat onto his face. Then he would dip his greasy fingers into a bag of powdered paint and rub the paint evenly over his face. Afterward, his whole body might be painted, and his fingernails might be drawn through the paint to produce a peculiar barred appearance.

Painting one's face and body was also a favorite way of mental conditioning. Native American warriors always painted themselves with their personal protective designs when they went to war (which also helped the war chief tell them apart), yet one must remember that all Native American paint cannot properly be called "war paint" since it was

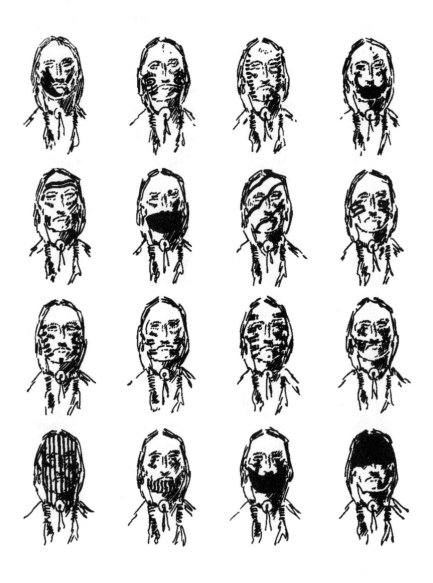

Typical ways of applying face paint, taken from the paintings and drawings of George Catlin, 1830s.

frequently used for purposes in no way connected with war. Designs of various kinds were used to designate membership in societies, when participating in ceremonies, as marks of achievement, and in mourning for the dead.

Bodies were painted in much the same manner and colors as faces, except that the lines were larger and more often wavy. When mixed with grease, the paints would remain on the body for a long time, for the Native American was often in a situation wherein he could not wash himself, or preferred, after a great victory or a ceremonial event, to leave the paint on as a reminder.

It might be assumed that face and body painting was done without reference to a particular design, and in fact early travelers often decided that the sole intent seemed to be for Native Americans to make themselves "as hideously ugly as possible." Yet such an approach would have been contrary to the Native American's nature, and indeed it is contradicted by better-informed authorities. With few exceptions the Native Americans' colors and patterns were harmonious, balanced, beautiful, and exciting. And it would be helpful if the Native American self-painting displayed in public ceremonies today was as well planned, executed, and explained. This is adequately borne out when one considers ceremonial self-painting in terms of the ancient Sioux attitude. They believed that by being painted, people had been changed. (Brown, *The Sacred Pipe*, p. 110) The painted ones had undergone a new birth, and with this had assumed new responsibilities, new obligations, and a new relationship. Therefore, ceremonial painting was to be done in a place hidden from the people, so that those painted would come forth as they did from the sweat lodge, pure, free of ignorance, and parted from the

Tatoo designs. *Left,* Omaha warrior. *Right,* Cree warrior.

troubles of the past. For the moment they were one with the Spirit, and a new relationship had been made.

In speaking of the use of blue paint, Black Elk said it was "very important and very sacred." (Brown, p. 123) Like Linderman, he explained that the power of a thing or act was in the understanding of its meaning. Thus by placing blue, the color of the heavens, upon tobacco, which represented the earth, he united heaven and earth and made them one. The red line every woman placed in the part of her hair tied her in with the earth, where everything lives and increases. Once again, one is greatly impressed with the spiritual depths of the Native American mind.

As the practice continued to evolve over the years, Plains painting became absolutely spectacular. In describing a meeting with some splendid Cheyenne who were in search of adventure, Father Nicholas Point reported that their hair was dressed with a sort of red earth; faces were painted blue, red, white, yellow, or even black; garments were decorated with porcupine quills and glass beads; hair was spread fanwise on the shoulders, flat on the brow, and hanging in long braids. And their heads were adorned with two feathers, extending vertically above the eyes. (Point, *Wilderness Kingdom*, p. 31)

Among the Omaha people, a leader of a war party painted diagonal lines on his face from the bottom of the eyes to the neck. The lines represented the path of his tears while "crying for the success of the expedition." Indeed, all war paint was applied after the nature of an appeal or prayer. Returning warriors of tribes who had taken scalps painted their faces black before entering their home village. The Crows said that black indicated the fires of revenge which had burned out with the completion of the raid. Pawnee scouts painted their faces white to symbolize the wolf, whose medicine was considered to be of the greatest help in scouting. The Kiowas often painted their body, horse, and shield with the same color either as an over-all pattern or as a more concentrated heraldic design. One Sioux warrior painted his body and his shield sky blue overlaid with large red dots! Red paint was generally applied to the face of persons taking part in ceremonies or who were being initiated into societies. Animal figures were sometimes drawn on the body to indicate the main helper of the clan or society to which the person belonged. Warriors returning from a victorious battle sometimes daubed their robes and blankets with buffalo blood, yet even this was so carefully done it would tell a story the entire camp could read. St. Clair discovered some very important things about the complexity of the body painting of the Wind River Shoshones. (Lowie, *The Northern Shoshone*, p. 233) He found that Wolf Dancers had realistic representations of bears or snakes below their breasts which stood for Bear or Snake Medicine, while a Sun Dancer had a similar chest painting of a buffalo. Right angles or angular horseshoes represented horse tracks; wavy lines extending along the entire length of the arms and legs symbolized the rainbow; short lines, horizontal, curved, oblique, or vertical, indicated people killed; and painted hands recorded hand-to-hand encounters with the enemy.

Tattooing was also a common practice on the Plains. The Wichitas did a great deal of it, and so did the other southern tribes. An Omaha leader could gain prestige for himself and for a daughter recently come of age by having her tattooed in the center of the forehead with a black circle representing the sun, and with a four-pointed star on her chest to symbolize the night. These designs symbolized his own war honors. An Osage man who had distinguished himself in war could also tattoo himself and his wife with a standard V-shaped design. An old Hidatsa man of the northern Plains was seen with a tattoo on one half of his chest. The Crows sometimes tattooed both sexes; and the Crees commonly tattooed both men and women. The men did this on their face, arms, and chests, while the women were only marked in the space between their lips and chin. Osage information reveals that the custom had ritualistic and social aspects in addition to its aesthetic purposes.

Quillwork and Beadwork

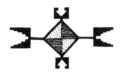

Quilling, which was the ancient forerunner of Plains beadwork, was found to be in complete harmony with Native American design attitudes, and it became the highest attainment of the female arts. It demanded a maximum in sensitiveness and great dexterity, but once applied, the sewn quills presented a smooth, strawlike surface, and were well suited to the popular geometric art of the Plains. The finest porcupine quills were used for amazingly delicate work, such as on special ceremonial moccasins, and some of the Native American women's achievements with these were so exquisite they resembled the sublime moose hair embroidery done by the Native Americans of the north and east, and from which they could only be distinguished by the shiny surface of the quills. It is generally conceded that the Sioux, Cheyenne, and Arapaho were the best quillers, and that most of the extreme southern tribes did not use quills at all. The Sioux explained the origin of quillwork by a legend of a mythical "double woman," who came in a dream to some woman who was a twin, to teach her the use of quills. She in turn taught other women how to use the quills, and associations of quillworkers or quilling societies were formed. They met at regular intervals to exhibit and talk over their work and explain how they did it.

Feasts were held and gifts were distributed. The quill designs made by each were considered her personal property and were not copied; for her designs were those which she was supposed to have dreamed and to which she could claim ownership. (Lyford, *Quill and Beadwork of the Western Sioux,* p. 40)

The American porcupine made his home in parts of Canada and Alaska, and the mountainous country of the northern and eastern United States. In the east he inhabited parts of Vermont, New York, and Pennsylvania, but porcupines were not found at all in most of the Plains country. The border line of their range followed the western edge of the Great Lakes country, swung up into Alberta, Canada, and then down through eastern Montana and Wyoming. Therefore, the majority of the Plains tribes had to obtain their quills by trade with the northernmost tribes.

The quill of the porcupine is a smooth, round, hollow tube with a sharp, barbed point at one end. It is white for about four fifths of its length, ending in a brownish-gray tip. Quills differ in length, thickness, and stiffness, being from one to four inches long, and from one sixteenth to three thirty seconds of an inch in diameter. The Plains quillworkers graded them into three sizes: the largest, which were those from the back; the slender, which were delicate quills from the neck; and the finest, which came from the belly. The medium-sized and coarser quills were used on the larger pieces. Quills were sorted as to size and color, and kept in small oval containers which were made of the intestines of an elk, of a buffalo bladder, or of rawhide. The waterproof bladder cases were usually decorated in a simple way with quill embroidery and later with beadwork.

Map showing approximate area of northern Plains where tribes employed porcupine quillwork. Adapted from "Quill and Beadwork of the Western Sioux," Department of Interior, 1940.

Dye colors and hues for the quills were obtained by boiling roots or berries. Red came from the snakeberry root, the buffalo or squaw berry. Yellow came from the huckleberry root, wild sunflower or cornflower petals—boiled with decayed oak bark or cattail roots. A purplish black was derived from the fox grape or black walnuts. Green dye was secured from a root, but the exact root is not known today. Later on blue was obtained from a clay procured through trade with the Whites. The quills were soaked briefly in clear water before they were immersed in the dye. The quills were boiled in the dye, then allowed to remain in the dye for only a short time, since if the quills remained in the dye too long the core of the quill would be soaked out. When the color was satisfactory, the quills were removed and placed on a piece of wood to dry.

Quills were washed well before the actual quilling began. For embroidery work the quillworker moistened and softened them by holding them in her mouth. She kept a number in one cheek, with the points protruding from her lips, and pulled out a quill as it was needed. It seems the saliva contained some special property which made the quills more pliable. After they had been softened in this way, the quills were flattened by drawing them between the fingernails or the teeth. The Sioux and the Arapaho smoothed the sewn quills further by rubbing them with a "quill flattener," which was a special tool made of a smooth, flat bone. The quiller's simple outfit included only the flattener, wood or bone awls, sinew, and a bone marker for tracing designs.

Quills were used in four principal ways: wrapping, braiding or plaiting, sewing, and weaving.

Wrapping was the simplest method of applying quills. It was used to cover long, slender objects like pipestems and leather fringes, and to bind strands of hair together. The method was to wrap the moistened quills around the item to be decorated, beginning with several overlapping rounds. As new quills were added, their ends were twisted around a previously applied quill with a half turn, and the turn was then concealed by the next quill.

Plaiting produced a more elaborate quill covering for such things as pipestems and ceremonial staffs than wrapping did. There was single-quill plaiting and two-quill plaiting. Both methods resulted in an overlapping and intertwined pattern looking like a series of small diamonds.

Since holes could not be made in quills without splitting them, quills were attached to buckskin or cloth by working a sinew thread back and forth through the material, and then winding or folding the soft, moistened quills over the exposed part of the thread. Once

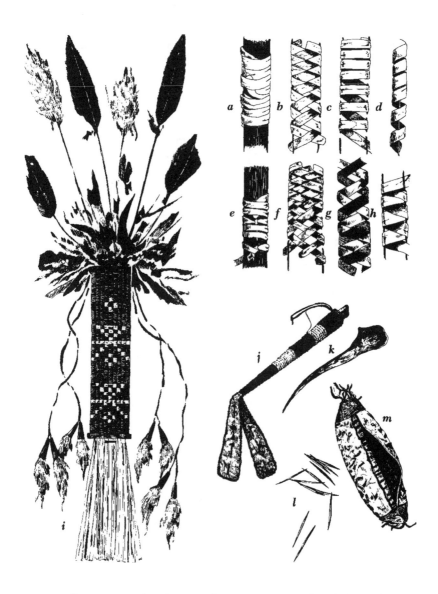

a, quill wrapping on hair. b, two-quill weaving. c, one quill applied straight. d, quill on single thread. e, quill wrapping without thread fastening. f, quill splicing. g, two-quill diagonal. h, quill on two threads. i, quilled hair ornament worn on back of warrior's head. j, beaded awl case and bone awl. k, bone awl. l, quills. m, bladder bag used for storing quills.

the quills dried, they remained firmly in position. The quills covered the thread, and when the work was completed none of the threads could be seen.

Weaving was accomplished by interweaving the quills in an over and under fashion each time they crossed. Once again a diamond-shaped pattern was produced.

The shortness of the quills led to designs which were made up of narrow bands. In a single strip the colors were varied according to a regular formula, and larger designs were made up by placing a number of bands side by side. Most quill patterns consisted of straight lines, but disks and flowers were also made for decorations on shirts, leggings, moccasins, and tipis.

Insofar as the four techniques were concerned, each Plains region had its own methods and selections of ways. For example, the western Sioux employed only the first three ways, and weaving was practiced chiefly by the Canadian Woodland Indians to the northeast of the Sioux.

With the advent of the brightly colored trade beads, quillwork gradually disappeared from many parts of the Plains. Along with it went the specific knowledge of the source and methods of preparation of many of the native vegetable dyes. Aniline dyes, carried west by the traders, were substituted for native dyes beginning about 1860, and the Native Americans of the reservation soon forgot how to make the native ones. Looking at the quilled pieces in museums today, one marvels at how these ancient dyes have weathered the ravages of time, for most are still so bright that they must have been radiant when they were first used. Collectors seek diligently for the relatively few quilled pieces still in existence, and even a small strip of the exquisite quilling brings an astounding price!

Before the European traders came to the Plains country with their glass beads, a relatively few crude native beads were fashioned out of shell, stone, bones of fish and animals, deer hoofs or toes, teeth, and seeds. There was also a tubular bone bead which was used for earrings and in making breastplates.

Most of these ancient beads were so difficult to make, however, that beadworkers were delighted to replace them with the abundant, bright, manufactured beads of glass and metal which were first brought into this country from Venice and Bohemia.

Sometime between 1800 and 1840, a large, opaque, irregular china bead was brought to the Plains. It was known as the pony bead because it was carried in by the pony pack trains. It was made in Venice, and was about one-eighth inch in diameter, or about twice as large as the beads used later. White and medium sky blue were the most used colors, but black beads also appeared in the old pieces, as did a few deep buff, light and dark red, and dark blue beads.

The beads were usually sewn onto skin strips, which were in turn sewn to the larger items to be decorated, but they were also applied directly to the item. The dominant technique employed was "lazy stitch" sewing, which affected the style since it virtually eliminated curved patterns. The straightforward designs worked out in this period were common to most of the tribes. They included narrow triangles, generally standing on or hanging from a horizontal bar; soldierlike rows of right-angled triangles; bands and rectangles; and assemblages of rectangles or straight bands. The impression conveyed was one of geometric simplicity. The beaded areas were quite narrow, with even six-inch-wide

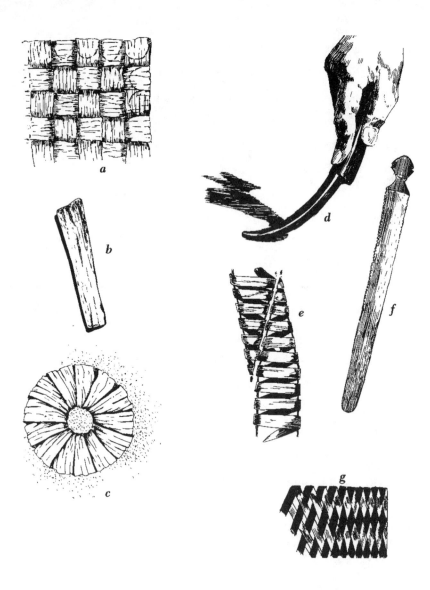

a, checker weave quill pattern. *b*, bone marker for incising pattern lines. *c*, rosette quill work. *d*, Blackfoot bone quill-flattener. *e*, method of butting two-thread quill patterns together. *f*, Arapaho bone quill-flattener. *g*, plaited quills.

bands being infrequent. Examples of original work with pony beads were among the articles collected by Lewis and Clark in 1805.

A smaller, round, opaque Venetian bead known as a "seed" bead reached the Native Americans about 1840. These were traded in a great variety of colors in bunches of five or six strings each, the strings varying in length from four to six inches. Seed beads were from one sixteenth to three sixteenths of an inch in diameter. In each case the delicacy of the pattern to be embroidered determined the size of the bead chosen. Because seed beads were partly made by hand they were somewhat irregular in shape, and the beadworkers found it necessary to exercise great care in selecting those of equal size. The colors of the first seed beads were richer and softer than the colors of subsequent batches, although the latter became more regular in size. The first seed bead period brought a design shift which emphasized simple triangles, often edged with steps.

When White settlers began to crowd into the Sioux country around 1860, beadwork became a major industry. Women began to cover their possessions with huge all-over patterns. They also did beadwork for the Whites, who sometimes supplied the garment to be decorated and dictated the style. Later, the traders imported Czechoslovakian beads, which were a trifle darker than the Venetian beads and inclined toward a slightly bluish tinge. One acquainted with both types of beads can recognize this coloring and guess very close to the date of the article. About 1870 translucent beads arrived, and toward 1885 beads which were colored with silver or gilt and faceted throughout. By now there was a huge variety of colors and sizes flooding into Native American country from Venice, Bohemia, France, and England.

What is called "the modern style" of beadwork came into being between 1870 and lasted till 1900. Its involved design character easily indicates the age of the decorated pieces. Truly individual tribal approaches manifested themselves in this period. The Sioux, Cheyenne, and Arapaho confined themselves to the lazy stitch; the Blackfoot, Sarsi, Plains Crees, and Flatheads made exclusive use of the overlay. The Crows, Assiniboines, Gros Ventres, and Plains Shoshones employed and combined both techniques. In the south, where beadwork was used only for trimming, the lazy stitch was in vogue among the Pawnees, whereas the Omahas preferred the overlay.

The ornamentation style of long, narrow strips, such as those used on leggings, remained somewhat uniform throughout the area, but observable differences continued to evolve in the decoration of items. For instance, Crow beadwork often had a narrow white border and checker patterns, and employed favored subtle colors such as violet. Sioux work emphasized large white or blue backgrounds, together with designs which had four or six points. Blackfoot designs had few white backgrounds and were very bold and simple with strong color contrasts. Southern Cheyenne garments had little of the usual beadwork on them and could often be identified by the large berry beads which were used. Floral patterns are usually Crow, Sioux, Blackfoot or southeastern tribes, and are of late-nineteenth-century vintage. The Shoshones were fond of blue-gray beads. A feature of northern beading which was easily recognized was that of coating the beads on clubs and targets with glue, so that they were firmly fixed to the item which was beaded. This was a custom followed by the Blackfoot and the Cree tribes.

Sioux beadworkers named their designs after natural objects which

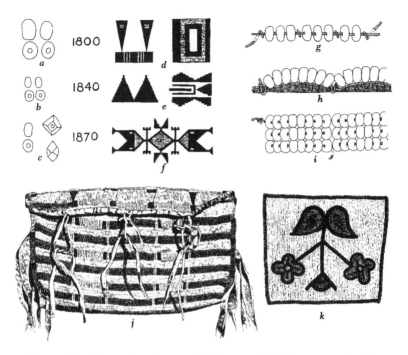

Types of beads introduced at certain dates on the Plains. *a*, pony beads, 1800-40. *b*, seed beads, 1840. *c*, medium-sized beads—richer colors, translucent, faceted, 1870 on. Typical Sioux designs which accompanied the bead periods. *d*, 1800-40. *e*, 1840-70. *f*, 1870 on. Types of bead stitches employed. *g*, the overlay. *h*, section through lazy stitch. *i*, top view of lazy stitch. *j*, beaded Crow saddlebag. *k*, example of Sioux overlaid stitch.

they resembled, and frequently used a design to symbolize some mystic idea or tribal scene. Hence designs had a general meaning, but there was no "language in beadwork" which told a story so legible the average Native American, apart from its owner, would understand it. A design that signified arrow points to one woman could be tipis for another—or anything else which had a triangular shape.

Some designs were used for male objects only, while others were used for the female. Carefully selected designs were used on articles provided for ceremonies and societies. Beaded designs were always distinct from the types of symbols painted on rawhide or buckskin.

Most articles were decorated with a design which bore a close relationship to the owner and use of the article. Pipes indicated a pipeholder, a warrior who had led one or more raids, and thus "carried the pipe." A feather embroidered on a warrior's pipe bag revealed his right to wear a real eagle feather in warfare. A horse track, patterned after the hoofprint of a horse, would be used to show that a man had captured horses from the enemy. The track was usually constructed of straight lines, although sometimes the connected end was curved like the regular hoof of a horse. Turtle emblems were placed on the small "Sand Lizards," bags which held a piece of a child's umbilical cord, and also on the yoke of a woman's dress and leggings and on baby cradles. The U-shaped design below the yoke of the woman's dress represented the breast of a turtle, while the winglike extensions corresponded to the sides of his shell. Used in this way the turtle design was believed to have power over the diseases peculiar to women, and also control over birth and infancy. Some have believed that turtle designs were only worn by women, but many male garments carry the design. Buffalo headdresses often had turtle designs painted on them or had small beaded turtle effigies appended to them. A spider web design placed on the robe of a child by a medicine woman invoked supernatural protection for the wearer. Some tribes regarded the spider as a mythological instructor of women in the art of embroidery.

A special design might be composed and adopted by any person as the result of a vision or of some important event or exploit. For example, an eagle design might be chosen to indicate proven leadership, while a tomahawk or bow and arrow would represent the fearless feats of a great warrior.

As symbolism often dictated the choice of designs, so too it influenced the selection of the colors which made up the design. Accordingly the colors came to have their own meanings, although the meanings did vary somewhat from tribe to tribe. White might signify winter. But white was also related to personal qualities such as purity, and to animals which were consecrated, such as buffalo, deer, rabbits, and birds.

Sky blue might represent a body of water in which the sky was reflected. It also meant sky, haze, smoke, distant mountains, rocks, and night. Navy blue and black sometimes indicated victory or enemies killed. In ceremonial use, blue represented many things: the sky, clouds, wind, the west, lightning, thunder, the moon, water, and day. Black often portrayed the night.

Red beads on a weapon might symbolize wounds inflicted; on a coat, wounds received. One or more horizontal red lines in the design of an eagle feather whose quill was wrapped with beads depicted the number of battles in which its owner warrior had taken part. In ceremonial use, red might indicate sunset, thunder, lightning, or forms of plant and animal life. Red lines often meant longevity, for red was commonly known as the life span color, or "trail on which woman travels," and was especially symbolic of that portion of a woman's life during which children might be born. Red was used for the ownership of property, and figured prominently in the Tobacco Societies.

Yellow was used for sunlight, dawn, clouds, or earth, and the Cheyenne loved it.

Green portrayed summer, vegetation, and new life. The Cheyenne

a, beaded Sioux blanket strip. *b*, Sioux quilled shoulder and arm bands for warrior's shirt. *c*, beaded feather and morning star designs on front and back of same shirt. *d*, quilled design used on front and back of man's war shirt. *e*, beaded designs used on Sioux pipe bags. *f*, Blackfoot warrior wearing blanket with beaded blanket strip.

were fond of it too.

By 1900 the great period of beadwork was over, and the technical skill which had been engendered and handed down from generation to generation virtually disappeared for a time from view. This period ended with some truly sensational creations, all of which are avidly sought after by museums and collectors. Some of the finest pieces of the last days were women's belts and dresses, bags, war clubs, beaded tomahawks, and items of horse gear. No other culture has ever matched the Native Americans' skill in beading, and without the deep spiritual approach and purposes to guide their hands even the later Plains Indians failed to equal the quality of the ancient work, although heartening signs of a renaissance can be seen in the products found in a few contemporary trading posts and stores.

Shields

As the eagle's-feather head-dress is the acme of all personal adorn-ment, so the shield is the head and front, the topmost summit of warlike paraphernalia. On it the warrior bestows infinite patience, care and thought. Not only must it be perfect in shape, in fit, in make, but also in its "medicine." He thinks it over, he works it over, he prays over it; to its care and protection he commends his life; to its adornment he elaborates thought, and devotes his time and means; to it he appends his "medicine bag" and the scalps of his enemies; on its front is painted his totem; it occupies a conspicuous but safe place in his lodge, and is hung out every fair day *in front of* his door; it is his shield, his protector, his escutcheon, his medicine, almost his God.

Dodge, *33 Years Among Our Wild Indians,* p. 422

In *Memories of Life Among the Indians,* by James Willard Schultz, the story is told how a Blackfoot named Fox Eyes came to make his shield. It's a superb story, and it touches upon many of the delightful and mysterious parts of shield making.

After several days of fasting, Fox Eyes had a vision experience of "a certain water animal," who had come to be his sacred helper. He returned to camp and shortly thereafter gave a feast, to which he invited several warriors, including some sacred-pipe men who were believed to be especially favored by "Sun."

Fox Eyes explained he now had a secret helper but needed a shield to go to war. Now he wanted to know who would make one for him if he provided the material.

Black Otter offered first, and was chosen for the honor. Fox Eyes promised him two horses to show his gratitude, since, as Schultz explains, shields were the Blackfeet's "most cherished, believed-to-be protective possessions."

The first requirement was golden eagle tail feathers with shiny black tips, so Fox Eyes built his eagle pit, and within ten days' time he had the tail feathers of four eagles. Everyone said this was "wonderfully good luck, since he now had enough to decorate the shield and to make a war bonnet, too." After this he went hunting with Schultz, and killed a buffalo bull. It was an old, old one, "whose once crescent-shaped, smooth, black, sharp horns were now mere rough, pale stubs."

This was the best possible evidence he had been brave: "He has fought many battles and survived them," said Fox Eyes as he and Schultz were removing the hide from its neck and shoulders. It was surely a sign that a shield made of his hide would be his powerful protector, and would keep him safe in battles with the enemies of his tribe.

They then took the piece of thick hide to Badger Woman, and she carefully removed its fur, leaving the glossy, brownish-black surface intact. Sometime later, it was handed to Black Otter, and the interesting ceremony of transforming it into a shield began to take place.

For this great occasion Black Otter dressed himself in his finest war clothes: soft buckskin shirt, leggings, moccasins, all of which were beautifully embroidered with multicolored porcupine quill designs. On

Shield types common to the northern Crow/Sioux area. *Left,* has three stuffed weasels and eagle feathers appended, and duck symbols painted on it. *Right,* has two bear tracks and four directions symbol painted on it, with eagle talon and beaver tail appended.

his head was the stupendous Blackfoot horns-and-ermine-skins warbonnet. His hands and face were painted a dull red, the sacred color. By the side of his lodge the piece of bull hide was stretched and pegged to the ground, and kneeling on it, he began to pray, at the same time starting to cut from the hide a circular piece about four feet in diameter.

"Oh, Sun! Oh, Night Light! Morning Star! Oh, all you Above Ones," he chanted, "Listen and pity us this day. This shield that I am making, give it of your sacred power so that it will keep its owner safe in his encounters with the enemy. Oh, Above Ones! To all of us, men, women, children, give long good life, good health; help us to overcome our enemies who are ever seeking to destroy us."

Meanwhile, several women were heating a number of stones in a little fire, and near it a small pit had been dug in the ground. The women rolled some of the stones into it and covered them with a thin layer of loose earth. Then Black Otter, with the help of three war-clothed friends, laid the circular piece of hide over the pit, and with each of them inserting pegs one after the other into slits that had been cut at regular intervals along its edge, fastened it tightly to the ground. As each of Black Otter's warrior friends drove in his peg, he told of some fight with the foe in which he had been the victor and counted coup. Soon the hide began to shrink from the heat until it bent the pegs toward the center. As fast as they loosened, the three men helpers pulled them, and then drove them in again. Black Otter supervised every step of the work, often feeling of the hide to make sure that it did not burn, and calling for more hot rocks as they were needed.

In about an hour the hide had shrunk to about half its original diameter, "and," says Schultz, "it was at least an inch thick." During the

Black Otter cutting shield hide to prepare it for shrinking.

entire process Black Otter prayed frequently, and together with his helpers sang a number of sacred songs. Finally, the shrinking was completed, and Fox Eyes took the hide home and finished making a "beautiful, tail-feathers-shield of it." (Schultz, *Blackfeet and Buffalo,* p. 144-54)

Here then is a combination of people involved in a Blackfoot shield's construction. A friend chosen for the honor supervised the shrinking, and the owner finished it. Still others helped, including women.

A Sioux warrior, however, reported that he secured and prepared the hide himself, and the symbols were applied by a medicine man. A common Sioux practice as this last step was completed was for the warrior to sit before the holy man and recount his coups with small sticks, dropping one for each coup, while the holy man painted on designs, prayed over them, and sang war songs to affix their power permanently. His services in such cases were considered to be worth as many as two fine horses. (Hofsinde, *Indian Warriors and Their Weapons*, pp. 74–75)

Although it could be punctured by a direct blow, a shield struck at an angle was tough enough to deflect lances, arrows, or even a smooth-bore ball at midrange. And so the regal, smoked shield of buffalo bull hide was carried on raids and war parties by almost every Plains warrior. Furthermore, it was highly valued for its medicine power, and it was considered a most sacred and potent possession. Its painted symbols and the items appended to it had resulted from a vision, and in its manufacture and care the warrior bestowed intense selectivity, craftsmanship, and thought.

Paradoxically, to carry an especially fine one in battle was also something of a risk, as the shield-bearer became more conspicuous and a prize coup. Grand boasting was sure to follow a victory over such a foe. And what a sight it was for a mounted warrior to sweep into a fight with his shield feathers and long pendants trailing out like visible lines of speed. The paintings of Russell and Remington, most of all, capture the full effect of the shield and owner at their regal best.

Fox Eyes and warrior friends shrinking hide over hot stones to increase thickness.

Warrior counting his coups with sticks while holy man paints symbols on front of shield.

It might be assumed that the medicine power of the shield was contained in the designs painted on it and in its other decorations, but serious consideration of the origin and construction of shields reveals that in the Native American's mind their power came from the sum of every step involved. As they saw it, the completed shield was literally infused with prayer and "power," and this force could be brought to bear as a wall of defense and to radiate destruction at the enemy. The fact is that it worked, perhaps because the enemy believed it too and responded accordingly. Battles were often won or lost simply on a strategy of shield medicines.

The war shield is a perfect example of the mingling of practical experience and holiness in Native American thought. To the Native American mind, not only the shape and properties of the material imparted their protective value, but also the vision, helpers, incantations, and rituals used to sensitize the shield and its cover of elk skin or some other fine material. Shields and covers for any warrior had to be made, or at least considered, by pipe holders or medicine men. Everyone in the tribe knew that dreams or visions had entrusted these men with the holy power required and the ceremonies which must be used, such as purifications, prayers, songs, sacrifices, and rituals with specific symbolisms. The resultant symbols burned into and/or painted on the shields, and painted or beaded or quilled on the covers, as well as the feathers, tassels, and the many other ornaments hung from both, were all talismanic, and when added together gave the shields a cumulative power. It was this assembled power which the warrior believed would preserve him from harm when he carried the shield into battle.

Some shields performed so well they became prophets for war expeditions. A certain Crow war party was led by a man named Mountain Wind, who had a shield of great renown. When they were in sight of the Sioux, Mountain Wind stopped to talk to his medicine before the fight.

The shield had a figure of a man painted in blue on his face. He had large ears and held in his left hand a straight red stone pipe. The figure was in the center of the shield, and it was bordered around its rim with "beautiful eagle feathers that fluttered in the breeze."

Mountain Wind took the shield from its cover, and held it above his head. Then he began to sing a song the others could not understand. Four times he sang it, and ceased. Four times the others responded with the traditional Crow yell. By then Mountain Wind was staggering like a blind man who was dizzy, and he was singing softly to his medicine, his face not toward the enemy, but toward the rising sun. His shield was waving toward the sun like a man's hands when he asked what was going to happen.

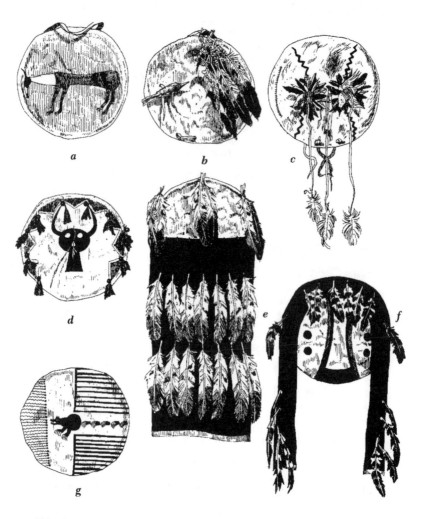

War shields, *a*, Crow shield with antelope symbol. *b*, Crow shield with stuffed bird on left and eagle feathers attached to small wooden stick on right. *c*, Crow shield with two small birds with feathers spread. *d*, Sioux shield with buffalo symbol and bells and clipped feathers around edge. *e*, Sioux shield with banks of eagle feathers attached to trade cloth apron. *f*, Sioux shield with typical trade felt trim to make streamers. *g*, Kiowa shield with bear symbols.

The others watched in utter fascination, even forgetting momentarily about the Sioux. Suddenly, Mountain Wind dropped the shield! It fell to the ground face downward. He lifted it as it had fallen, face downward, to the level of his breast, still singing his medicine song, and held it there till an eagle's feather fell fluttering from the shield's edge to the ground. Then Mountain Wind turned the shield to see its other side. He saw many Sioux scalps and many horses, but added that one great Crow warrior would not be going home with them. Immediately Long-horse began to sing, telling of his own foreboding dream, and that he was the one who would not return.

The Crows took nine Sioux scalps and all their horses on that raid. Long-horse was the only Crow to die by a Sioux hand! (Linderman, *Plenty Coups*, pp. 279-80)

Another story tells of a shield which its owner could roll along the ground and then prophesy by its condition and whichever side was face up upon falling what course to follow and what the result of a raid or battle would be. The impressive thing is that the predictions were so numerous and accurate as to merit everyone's attention and reflection. (Wildschut, *Crow Indian Medicine Bundles*, p. 72)

In some of the tribes, shields of a common design were carried by members of societies who also used virtually the same war dress, war cries, body paint, horse decorations, and songs. Sioux pictographic drawings reveal their commonly shared society symbols did not always include the shield, but it is said that among the Cheyenne all of the shields were made by one of the societies whose members carried a plain red shield with a buffalo tail hanging from it. These red shields were believed to be particularly powerful, for the pattern was supposed to have been handed down originally by the great prophet, Sweet Medicine, who brought the tribe its sacred medicine arrows. When swung in a circle before the enemy, the red shield bearers were convinced such powers would prevent enemy arrows from hitting either the shields or themselves. If the shields failed to prevent this, it was "obviously" due to some other failure than the shields'.

Designs were usually painted on both the front of the shield and on its soft buckskin cover (or covers). Some of the patterns contained pictures of animals and/or symbols of the elements, such as stars, or lightning, or other natural objects. Some of the designs painted on Comanche shields were lines so located as to serve as a compass to guide the owner on a cloudy day. A certain line was kept pointed at a distant landmark. All of the designs were special helpers given to the shield owner in his vision. Such designs were always applied in accordance with the strict ceremonies and taboos connected with the tribal traditions. And it was accepted that the violation of a single one would destroy the shield's power.

Bear Society members always had a bear on their shields, although an individual other than the society members might also use the symbol as the result of a vision. A drawing of a bear or bear footprint meant that the owner believed it would transfer to him the strength and abilities of that animal whenever they were needed. If a tortoise was included in the pattern, it was because the shieldbearer had been led to believe he would live a long life (that is, long enough to live through most battles—but not till he was toothless!). The tortoise was long-lived, and the warrior had seen that it would move about even though its head was cut off. Special medicines made of the whole or parts of "dream" animals or

a, Arikara shield with buffalo symbol and eagle tail feathers. *b*, Gros Ventre shield with stuffed hawk appended. *c*, circles on buffalo indicate areas reported by Native American authorities from which hide was taken for shields. *d*, tipi with tripod behind for sunning shield, and in which position shield protected rear of tipi through its infused power.

Steps in making shield by most common method. *a*, pit for fire. *b*, hide stretched and pegged over pit. *c*, heated rocks added. *d*, water poured on rocks to make steam. *e*, hair removed. *f*, shrunken hide pegged over mound to give dish shape. *g*, marking with charcoal to indicate finished shape.

Shield making continued. *h,* pounding hide for final shaping and smoothing. *i,* shoulder loop attached to back of shield through holes in shield. *j,* testing shield. *k,* shield cover, front and back view. *l,* painting symbols on shield proper.

birds were tied to the shield or placed under the outer cover, and long pendants of animal hides, soft buckskin, or blanket cloth, preferably red or blue and decorated with eagle feathers, were fastened to the shield itself. These were supposed to endow the warrior with the courage and abilities of those animals or birds. Naturally, an opponent could read the symbols as well as the owner, and the ensuing engagements became all the more interesting for it.

To make the standard shield in use on the Plains, a circular section of hide, approximately forty inches in diameter, was cut from the original piece taken from the buffalo bull. This was slightly more than twice as large as the shield was to be when finished. The average hide, after shrinking, was about seventeen inches in diameter, although they varied from twelve to twenty-six inches. The skin was also shrunk until it was almost twice its original thickness, or a half inch at its thickest point. It is said that "The shield was a good practical shield made from the breast or neck hide of a bull buffalo." The area indicated is under the neck and between the shoulders. But the assertion is made many times that the hide used for the shield actually came from the hump area, which was thick and tough. An Assiniboine clearly affirms this, stating that "shields for warfare were made from the thick hide that covers the hump of the buffalo." (Grant, *American Indians Yesterday and Today*, p. 285)

The hide was fastened down with wooden pegs over a round hole in the ground about eighteen inches in diameter by eighteen inches deep. One edge of the hide was left loose, and this was lifted from time to time and red-hot stones were dropped in the hole. Water was poured on the stones until the hot steam caused the hide to shrink to the desired size. The hair was then removed with a stone or bone scraper,

Alternate methods of shrinking hide. *a*, shrinking by layer of heated dirt. *b*, pit fire kept burning. *c*, steaming over hot stones. *d*, covering with thin layer of clay and hot coals. *e*, shrinking by use of heated rocks. *f*, method of making hoop shield, top view, *g*, back view, and *h*, cross section showing hide folded around wood hoop.

and the still soft hide was then pegged down over a small mound of earth. This gave it a dish shape which increased its strength. A circular shape was marked on the hide with a pointed stick which had been rubbed with charcoal, and the edges were trimmed smooth to this pattern. Finally, the shield was laid on a hard surface such as a piece of rawhide, and the wrinkles and dents were pounded with a smooth stone or berrymasher until the surface of the shield was fairly smooth.

A buckskin, rawhide, or other type of sling and a hand loop were then attached to the shield, and it was tested by having the warriors shoot arrows at it from a distance of twenty yards or so. If the arrows bounced back from the hide, leaving it neither penetrated nor injured, the shield was considered fit for use. If not, it was rejected and another made. (Salomon, *The Book of Indian Crafts and Indian Lore,* pp. 179-82)

Herman Lehmann relates how the Comanches taught him to ride wild horses, to jump from the ground onto a horse as he raced by and dodge an arrow at the same time. He was taught to crouch close to the neck of the horse so an enemy could not hit him, and how to use the shield to ward off arrows. He was given a shield and placed off about fifty yards. Four braves took bows and blunt arrows and began to shoot at him. He knew what he had to do, for he had seen the performance before. He began moving the shield up and down and from right to left. The arrows poured against it and he managed to ward some of them off with the wavy motion, but torrents of blunt sticks came and he was too slow. One passed just over the shield and struck him in the forehead. He saw stars—not those painted ones on the shield, but real fiery flashes—the arrow downed him, and those who were firing let up the shooting for a time. However, the target practice soon resumed, and he had to

Hoop shield details. *a*, method of measuring size of willow hoop. *b*, three fingers' width allowed around hoop to provide for hide to wrap over hoop. *c*, shrinking hide in hot water. *d*, punching holes in softened hide for lacing. *e*, method of lacing hide on hoop. *f*, close-up of lacing detail.

keep at it until he had learned how to use the shield. He was knocked down several times before he became adept. "All Indians," he said, "were thus trained." (Lehman, *Nine Years Among the Indians,* pp.25-27)

The decoration of the shield was always accompanied by special ceremonies conducted by medicine men and proven warriors. The cover of soft dressed skin, such as deer or elk, was generally made first. It was painted with a design different from but related by color or substance to that on the shield itself.

The front of the shield was painted after the cover was finished, and other decorations were attached to it, such as feathers, animal skins, birds, etc.

The foregoing was the most common method of making a shield, but there were a number of ways in which hides were shrunk to make shields both among the tribes and within a given tribe. They certainly illustrate the versatility of the Native American craftsmen.

In one method the hide was prepared by staking it down on the bottom of a hole six or eight inches deep and covering it with dirt. A fire was kept burning over it for several days. After this, the hide would be shrunken and very thick. Those relating the method do not explain how the Native American moved his stakes while they were covered with fire and hot dirt. Perhaps the fire could burn down and be removed at regular intervals once the Native American became familiar with the hide's rate of shrinkage. However, since it shrank rapidly, other methods seem easier by far. The pit hole would need to be as large in diameter as the original hide, though, and perhaps if the fire were only placed in the center and could still manage to shrink the hide, the stakes, being outside it, could be more easily reached. (Grant, p. 285)

In another method a man about to construct himself a shield dug a hole two feet deep and as large in diameter as he intended to make his shield. In this he built a fire. Over it, a few inches higher than the ground, he stretched the rawhide horizontally over the fire, using little pegs driven through holes made near the edges of the skin. Again, this skin was twice as large as the size of the finished shield. He invited his particular and best friends into a ring to dance and sing around it until the shrinking was completed, and to petition the Great Spirit to instill power into it. Then he spread glue made by boiling buffalo hoofs and joints in water, which was rubbed and dried in as the skin was heated. Meanwhile, a second man busily drove other pegs inside of those in the ground—as the first were gradually giving way and being pulled up by the contraction of the skin. (Catlin, Vol. I, p. 241)

In yet another method the rawhide was cut in a disk shape twice the size of the finished shield, and shrunk by steaming over hot stones. (Tunis, *Indians*, p. 100)

In another variation the hide was covered with a thin layer of clay on which burning coals were placed until the skin was shrunk and hardened. (Lowie, *The Northern Shoshone*, p. 193)

In a final method, a pit was dug, including an access trough on the side by which cold rocks could be removed and hot rocks added from time to time. The pit was filled with hot rocks and covered by a layer of dirt shaped to the curve the owner wanted his shield to be. Over this the hide was staked, with one edge loose and the pegs being moved in the conventional way as the hide shrunk. (Grinnell, *The Cheyenne Indians*, pp. 187-202)

An Arapaho states that he shrunk the hide for his shield by soaking

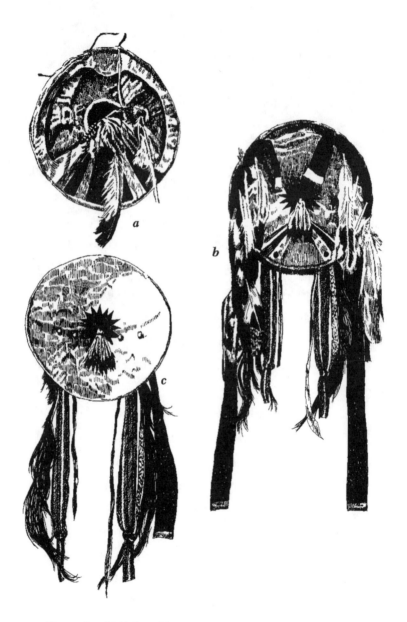

Comanche shield from Harvey collection. *a*, outer cover. *b*, inner cover. *c*, concave shield.

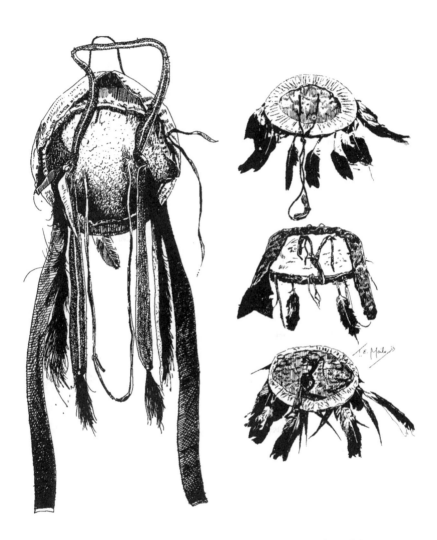

Left, back of Comanche shield. *Right*, backs of Plains shields from Gilcrease Institute collection.

it in water. This may account for the extremely wrinkled surfaces one sees on some shields. (Bass, *The Arapaho Way*, p. 33)

A second and less common kind of Plains shield was made with a wooden hoop for a frame.

The Sioux made it in the following way: A green, three-quarter-inch-diameter willow hoop was bent to a diameter approximately the width of a man's chest. The ends of the hoop were beveled, lapped, and lashed together with sinew. The buffalo hide was soaked in boiling water to shrink it (finished hoop shields were not as thick as the heat-shrunken self-shields which used no hoop). The hide was trimmed to the shape of the round hoop, allowing three fingers width of extra hide beyond the hoop, and holes or slits were punched at regular intervals around the edge of the hide. The hide was then pegged down over a mound of dirt to give it its concave shape. An alternate method of obtaining the shape was to form it by pressing the still soft skin down into a dished-out sand mold. The extra hide was then folded over the edges of the hoop and cross-laced through the slits to the frame. Shield lacings were thongs cut from heavy buckskin. The buckskin sling and hand loops were then attached in the traditional ways and the shield was tested. (Hassrick, *The Sioux*, p. 199)

Lightweight ceremonial dance shields were often made in this way, with the wooden hoop being removed after the hide had hardened. The back of the shield in such cases was interlaced with a buckskin thong after the manner employed for tightening shield covers.

The Comanches made the regular heat-shrunken shields, but they also made hoop shields by throwing the hide over a fire until it was hot enough to remove the meat. The hide was then worked with round stones until it was soft and sewed onto a rattan or hickory hoop. It was "dished" by stretching it over stakes until it was dry. (Lehman, pp. 25-26)

To speak of shields and their construction is one thing, to actually see them is another, since a beautifully crafted one is simply stupendous. From the collector's point of view it is regrettable that so many were buried with their owners, and thus deteriorated in the grave or on the burial platforms. Fred Harvey, who assembled one of the finest private collections of Plains and Southwest items ever known, obtained a heat-shrunken Comanche shield which deserves special mention.

This Comanche shield has not one, but two covers. It is concave, and thus provides a dish or basket to hold its beautiful pendants and array of eagle feathers. It is eighteen inches in diameter, and the total length from the top of the shield to the end of the wool pendants is fifty-two inches. The shield itself is approximately one-half inch thick.

The cap, or outer cover, has an inner circle of black bordered by white, the next area is deep blue, and the outer edge is lemon yellow. The radiating lines are alternately orange and black. A small group of feathers in the center of the cover is a combination of hawk and eagle wing feathers. One large eagle tail feather also hangs from the center and there are two smaller side feathers with breath feathers attached. The outer cap fits over the inside cover like a dust cover on a case. There are metal bells on it—which means it was used for ceremonial dances, and perhaps was not carried into enemy territory, where the noise of the bells would give the owner away.

The inside cover has the greatest number of eagle tail feathers attached to its front at each side, and also two long dark-blue blanket cloth pendants. Its center dishes in to fit the concave shape of the shield itself, and everything hanging on it packs into this dish receptacle so neatly it excites the utmost appreciation. Undoubtedly, this cover was carried to war, pointed toward the enemy to dispel its medicine, and then removed as an actual battle was engaged.

The shield itself was used for the fight. A war sling of buckskin is attached to the back, as is another sling of woven (Mexican origin) woolen material. This second band is four inches wide, and being more comfortable than the narrow buckskin sling was probably used to carry the shield to and from a raid. There are also two long pendant strips of buffalo skin, with hair, attached to the back of the shield.

According to the paintings of Russell, Remington, and Koerner, a warrior carried his shield on foot or horseback in several different ways. Ordinarily the loop of the shield was hung around the warrior's neck, and the shield itself was carried on his back. The quiver was carried horizontally underneath or below it. The shield loop was knotted in front to pull the shield snugly to the back to prevent loss or bouncing while traveling. During engagements, the shield was shifted to where it could be brought into play by the left arm, and raised or lowered to ward off arrows or bullets. Judging by most paintings and photographs, when not carried on the warrior's back, the shield was hung from the saddle cantle on the left side of the horse—again, with the loop knotted and the shield pulled snugly to the horse. The left side attachment was not an absolute, however, and some warriors hung them on the right. They were also hung from the pommel, and so were sometimes in front of and underneath the rider's legs.

The loop was usually attached to the back of the shield with its tie on the left back tie point placed a bit higher than the tie point on the

Crow warrior with full tail bonnet and war shield decorated with eagle tail feathers.

right. When carried over the shoulder this allowed the shield design itself to remain straight for the benefit of all who viewed it.

It is commonly believed that the shield front, or side held toward the enemy, was convex. Yet some shields in the Harvey Collection, the Gilcrease Institute, the Southwest Museum, and the San Diego Museum of Man are concave, as was the Comanche shield just mentioned. There are two reasons for this. The first is that a concave shield provided better deflection than a convex one, since an obstacle striking the loosely held shield caused it to yield and turn around the arm. The convex shield, in moving, tended to deflect the arrow or bullet into head or legs, whereas the concave shield provided a lip to help shunt them away. The second was that a concave shield provided a dish or basket into which the numerous feathers and other medicine items could be neatly packed or folded.

Museum shields are seldom smooth and round. Admittedly, some of them may have warped considerably over the years, yet at best they were irregular circles and of a somewhat uneven surface in the beginning. Shrinking and cutting and pounding such a heavy hide obviously had its difficulties and effect.

When not being carried by the warrior, the shield was placed outside the tipi on a sunny day on a tripod at the rear or west side. It was placed there as a bulwark to protect the lodge owner against attack or evil spirits approaching on his "blind" side. Blackfoot tipis often had two tripod racks behind them. One tripod held the shield and the other the medicine bundle. It was, however, equally common to place both on the same tripod. Placing the shield outside was called "sunning the shield," and the Native Americans believed that it was being further infused with power from the sun. The Kiowas said that anyone violating the taboos concerning the placement and care of shields was subject to certain disgrace and disaster. Drawings and paintings also show tripods of different heights, some not more than five feet, some ten or more feet tall. Photographs hit a mid-point, and are probably the best guide, indicating a tripod of seven or eight feet at its apex.

There were four types of shields which were used on the Plains: the dance shield, which was a lightweight version of the war shield; the medicine or holy man's shield; the miniature shield, which was a small copy of a warrior's war shield, and which he sometimes carried on long journeys in place of the war shield; and the war shield.

The war shield was made in three varieties. The least-used variety, and one which has not been described in the previous shield material, was made by stitching four or five layers of flat rawhide together, cutting these in the traditional round shape, and then decorating the front side of the hide with feathers and strips of cloth. A second variety was made by forming the hide around a wooden hoop. Many kinds of hoop shields were constructed, but these called for a thinner and weaker hide than those made by the third means, which was the heatshrinking process. Most war shields by far were fashioned this way, for the shrinking produced a thick hide and it was easier to press into a concave or convex shape which aided deflection.

Prior to the arrival of the horse, Plains war shields were quite large—often being three feet or more in diameter. These were much too cumbersome for mounted men, though, and so the size was reduced until the average war shield measured only eighteen inches in diameter.

Young men often went as initiates on their first or second raid without a shield. And men who journeyed on foot into enemy territory did not always carry heavy shields. But the shield was the final piece of equipment constructed by a young man preparing to take up his full adult responsibilities. He might make several more shields during his active period as a warrior, but the first one, coupled with his personal medicines, gave him the initial protection and confidence he needed to share the full responsibilities of a raid or war party to be carried out on horseback. He would also use the shield for defense if his village was attacked.

Medicine shields were usually covered with the most intriguing appendages and symbols, but the war shields were the truly sumptuous creations. Some of them would rank with the finest artworks of all time— and yet a shield was much more than a piece of art. To the Native American, a shield vibrated with power, and by sunning it, he could continue to draw power from above into it for an indefinite time. Small wonder then it was placed by his side to protect him when he made his final journey into the Mystery Land of the dead.